CONTENTS

ISBN: 0-87441-390-7

PUBLISHED BY BEHRMAN HOUSE, INC.

SPRINGFIELD, NEW JERSEY 07081

STUDY QUESTIONS BY DR. ROBERT L. PLATZNER

COVER/BOOK DESIGN BY ROBERT J. O'DELL

MANUFACTURED IN THE UNITED STATES OF AMERICA

INTRODUCTION

ALTHOUGH THE TORAH IS AT THE HEART OF WHAT A JEW studies, the book Jews have studied most, certainly in the last thousand years, is the Talmud. And the heart of the Talmud is the *Mishnah*, or Oral Law.

In one sense, the Torah provided the constitution of the ancient Jews. But the laws, the commandments, the Jews found in the Torah are quite different from laws passed by Congress or a modern legislature. A legislated law is as clear and specific as the writers of the law can make it. For example, a traffic law may say, "Any automobile, truck, bus, tractor, motorcycle, or other self-propelled vehicle which enters upon or crosses any street, highway, road, or public way . . . " Everything is spelled out in this law so that there can be no question about who is covered and what is permitted—or not permitted.

The commandments in the Torah are not, for the most part, specific at all. Even a law that appears to be perfectly simple: "You shall not murder," raises questions. When is a homicide a murder? Some commandments seem incomplete; others appear too general. And as always, in the development of people and nations, new situations arise to which none of the laws seems to apply.

Torah says, "You shall not wholly reap the corners of your field . . . you shall leave them for the poor and the stranger" [LEV. 19:10]. But how big is a corner? Is it enough to leave four stalks of corn? Ten? Who are the poor? Who is a stranger? Is a city dweller excused from caring for the poor and for strangers because he has no fields?

MAKING THE LAWS SPECIFIC

The Torah provided a way of making the laws specific:

"If there is a matter too hard for you in judgment, between blood and blood, between plea and plea, between stroke and stroke, even matters in controversy within your gates; then shall you arise . . . and you shall come to the priests, the Levites, and unto the judges that shall be in those days; and you shall inquire; and they shall declare unto you the judgment. And you shall do according to the judgment, which they shall declare unto you . . . and you shall observe to do according to all that they teach you." [DEUT. 17:8-10]

And if the judges disagreed among themselves, the Talmud said that the majority ruled: "Where there is a controversey between an individual and the many, the *halakhah* follows the many" [BER. 9a]. However, this ruling

3

was taken from the same verse of Talmud that said: "You shall not follow a multitude to do evil" [EXOD. 23:2].

The earliest judges were priests or elders of the tribes. Later they were scribes, and still later, rabbis. When a dispute was brought to them, they looked for the answer first in the Written Law, the Torah. If there was no clear answer in the Torah, they looked into the other books of Scripture for helpful passages. Generally, this search gave some clue to the correct answer. Then, out of their marvelous memories, the judges recalled similar cases decided by past judges. Based on Scripture and what had been decided in the past—called precedent—the judges made rulings.

So a second body of law developed, the Oral Law, which told the ancient Jews (and still tells us today) how much of a field is "corners," and who are the poor and the strangers who may eat of it. Through this Oral Law, the commandments of the Torah—the Written Law—were made to work for Jews who lived centuries after the original laws were developed. Thus a body of law first set down in the tenth century BCE could apply to Jews in the tenth century CE, and the twentieth too.

With each passing century, life became more complicated. What was simple when most Jews lived in villages, and tended flocks, and grew their own food, became involved when the villages became towns and most people began buying their food. Life became even more complicated when Jews no longer lived in or governed their own country, but, instead, lived under many different kings.

Take something as simple as working on the Sabbath, on which the Torah is quite clear:

"Six days shall you labor and do all your work; but the seventh day is a Sabbath unto the lord your God." [EXODUS 20:9-10]

"You shall keep the Sabbath therefore, for it is holy unto you." [EXODUS 31:14]

But how does one "keep" the Sabbath? It was a problem for farmers because animals had to be fed. It was an even greater problem for city dwellers who depended on services provided by others. Besides, what is considered work?

Torah lists only three specific kinds of work that could not be done on the Sabbath: kindling fire, traveling beyond "your place," and gathering wood. Further on in Scripture, Jeremiah and Nehemiah listed other kinds of work forbidden on the Sabbath: carrying a burden, making wine, loading a beast of burden, setting up a stall or store, selling things, and business in general. Surely, the ancient judges argued, this does not complete the list of things that are included in "work." A search of Torah gave them a more complete list. The chapters of the Book of Exodus that include the law against working on the Sabbath are followed by chapters describing the building of the Tabernacle. All the jobs necessary for building the Tabernacle are listed; and these became the jobs, or "work," that could not be done on the Sabbath. From then on, it was up to the judges, or rabbis, to decide about tasks not included in that original list.

Each century brought new questions about work. Three hundred years ago it was about iron smelting. The smelter fires could not be allowed to go out on the Sabbath without great damage and cost. A great scholar, Rabbi Meir Eisenstadt, ruled that this work should be permitted on Sabbath. And in our own century the question of electricity was raised: Is it work to push the button that causes electricity to do work? Authorities differed about this.

THE ORAL LAW GROWS

In the centuries before the Common Era, the Oral Law kept growing. As more and more questions were raised, more and more decisions were made, and more and more judgments handed down. In order to try a case properly, a judge had to know thousands of rulings made by rabbis in the past. Yet the Oral Law remained just that—oral; it was not written. It was passed along by word of mouth from one generation of rabbis and scholars to the next.

There was no commandment that said the Oral Law could not be written down; only tradition implied that it couldn't. But the rabbis were fearful and resisted writing it down for two very important reasons. According to Scripture, the Written Law or Torah was given to Moses already written down. This was God's Law; it could not be changed, subtracted from, or added to. The Oral Law is really an *interpretation* of this Written Law. If this second body of law was also written, the two might be confused. Some people might say, "See, it is written thus and so...." and they might use the written Oral Law rather than the Torah as the final word. But only the Torah was *The* Word of God.

The second reason why the rabbis resisted writing the Oral Law was equally important. Oral Law made the Torah work whatever the century and whoever the king. Oral Law had to be very flexible. Persia ruled Israel, then the Egyptians, who succumbed to the Greeks. The Romans took over after the Greeks. These changes didn't bother the Jews too much as long as they were allowed to live by their own law—which of course adjusted to the differences in Roman, Greek, and Egyptian rule. But changing a body of oral law is a lot simpler than changing a law book. There was the danger, the rabbis said, that Oral Law, once put on paper, would become as fixed as Written Law.

Then came events that forced a change in the thousand-year rule against writing down the Oral Law. In the seventy years between 65 CE and 135 CE, the Jews fought three wars against the might of Imperial Rome. They lost all three, and at the end Israel was no longer the home of the majority of Jews.

The Jews had always been great travelers and settlers. They had set up colonies throughout the known world even during the many centuries they lived in Israel. There were Jewish settlements from Spain in the west, to India in the east, and from Germany in the north, to Ethiopia in the south. No matter where they lived, the Jews had a homeland, a place they could look to for religious and legal authority. But, after the last disastrous revolt against Rome, there was no more Israel, there was no more Jerusalem, there was no more legal authority in the homeland. A small Jewish colony remained in Roman Palestine, but most Jews lived outside the Land. The center of Jewish life and authority moved to Babylon.

Scattering of the Jews created a big problem. How were the Jews of Babylon, Alexandria, and Rome supposed to follow the same law when much of that law was only in the memories of scholars and judges? If there was no central authority for the law, then there would soon be a Roman Jewish law, an Egyptian Jewish law, and a Babylonian Jewish law. A change had to be made.

THE ORAL LAW WRITTEN DOWN

Around 200 CE, the Oral Law was written down. It remained the Oral Law, different from the Written Law, but it was now on paper (or parchment) as the written Oral Law. The change was started by Judah haNasi (Judah the Prince or Governor), head of the Jewish community of Palestine.

This change didn't come suddenly. It had been in preparation for more than two hundred years. Great scholars had already divided the great mass of Oral Law into criminal law, civil law, family law, agricultural law, and religious law. They did this, at first, to make it easier to remember. A judge who specialized in criminal law didn't have to remember every case in family law. A specialist in religious law didn't have to know all about agricultural law. Along the way, scholars had organized all the Oral Law into logical divisions.

These codes of the Oral Law are called *mishnah*, from the Hebrew word *shonah*, "to repeat." A *mishnah* is a repetition of the Oral Law. A *mishnah* is also a single rule or decision; in the plural they are called *mishnayot*. The *Mishnah*, with a capital "M," is the whole body of Oral Law collected by Rabbi Judah haNasi.

When Rabbi Judah began putting together his *Mishnah*, he had over a dozen earlier collections of law before him. He took from each, but mostly from the *mishnah* of Rabbi Akiba, which had been perfected by Akiba's disciple, Rabbi Meir.

Rabbi Judah collected thousands of rulings and decisions made over many, many generations. He chose among the different interpretations of the same Torah commandment; he arranged all the materials into a system; he summarized the arguments of the judges and rabbis; he threw out what seemed unimportant or repetitious. He also added his own rulings where questions were not answered clearly.

Rabbi Judah did all this without changing the material. Wherever possible, he repeated arguments and decisions in the words of the original judge. And where there were differences of opinion, he didn't decide who was right. Rabbi Judah did not assume he was wiser than those rabbis who first heard the case. He included both the majority opinion and the minority opinion in his *Mishnah*, even if the minority was a minority of one.

Most of the decisions are labeled. That is, the name of the rabbi who made the decision is given, and if there are several decisions, the name of each judge is attached to his decision. All together, one hundred fifty-eight rabbis and scholars are mentioned by name in the *Mishnah*.

The rabbis mentioned in the *Mishnah* are the *Tannaim* (singular, *Tanna*), from the Aramaic word *teni*, meaning "to hand down orally," or "to teach." Most of the *Tannaim* are mentioned only once or twice in the *Mishnah;* some are mentioned several times. These twelve rabbis are quoted frequently:

Rabbi Akiba	Joshua ben Hananiah
Eleazar ben Azariah	Judah ben Ilai
Gamaliel II (called Rabban)	Rabbi Meir
Ishmael ben Elisha	Simeon ben Gamaliel
Johanan ben Nuri	Simeon ben Yohai
Yose ben Halafta	Rabbi Tarphon

The Jews of the time when the *Mishnah* was being put together spoke Aramaic in their daily lives. This meant that the decisions of the rabbis and judges in cases brought before them were given in Aramaic. But the language of the *Mishnah* is Hebrew. This is probably because Rabbi Judah was a very strong and strict Hebraist. It was said that even the maids in his home had to speak Hebrew. And Hebrew gave the *Mishnah* greater authority because Hebrew was the language of the Written Law.

The *Mishnah* is a big book. In the English translation it is more than eight hundred pages. But it is obvious that Rabbi Judah could not possibly have included, in his *Mishnah*, all the rulings and decisions made over many centuries of Oral Law. Some rulings had to be left out. Most of these "left out" decisions were lost as scholars forgot them; but many were remembered long enough to be included later in the Talmud. These are the *beraitot* (singular, *baraita*), from the Aramaic word meaning "outside."

ON THE ONE HAND, ON THE OTHER HAND

The law books of nations are books of yeses and noes: This you may do, this you may not do. the law book of the Jews, the *Mishnah*, has very few yeses or noes. It is a book of cases and decisions made by judges on those cases. Some cases were decided unanimously: All the judges agreed. Some decisions were split: Some judges say yes and some say no; some may even say maybe. The *Mishnah* reports all the decisions. If necessary, the minority opinion is given as much room as the majority opinion. The *Tannaim* never forgot that Oral Law, although it was written down, was flexible. It had to have room to change as the world changed. Of course, they put it differently; They said that perhaps wiser scholars may find a new insight. No one knew when a minority opinion might become the majority opinion.

The judges tried to make their decisions according to some commandment in the Torah, or an interpretation of some commandment, or an interpretation of something in the *Tanakh*. However, wherever there are interpretations, there are differences among interpreters. (It is the same among the judges who interpret the United States Constitution.)

Most of the decisions of the *Tannaim* could be based on a passage of Scripture, generally by adding specifics—like saying exactly what kind of work is meant by the law against work on the Sabbath. The general commandment to leave the corners of the field to the poor and to strangers was easily interpreted by defining a corner, the poor, and strangers. But not all commandments could be brought up-to-date so easily. Some commandments just weren't workable centuries after they were written. Some laws laid down in the sixth century BCE were impossible to enforce five or six hundred years later.

Still, no judge, no *Tanna*, not even a king could deny the Torah or change any part of the Written Law. If it was in the Torah, it had to be followed. So the judges interpreted some laws in such a way as to make them impossible to enforce—without denying the commandment.

For example, it is a commandment that if a son is "stubborn and rebellious, he does not hearken to our [the parents'] voice; [if] he is a glutton and a drunkard," he shall be put to death [DEUT. 21:20-21]. Such a law may have made sense when Judah and Israel were fighting Assyrians, Babylonians, and each other. But such a law could not be enforced in the more civilized second century CE. Yet the law was Torah; it could not be changed. Nor did the later judges change it; they defined who was a rebellious son, and what was meant by a glutton and a drunkard.

A rebellious son, said the rabbis, had to be over thirteen; if he was under thirteen he was not responsible for his actions. On the other hand, he couldn't be much older than thirteen because he would then be a man and would not have to obey his parents in all things. That left little time for rebellion as a capital crime.

A glutton, said the rabbis, was someone who ate at least one pound of meat at one sitting. If the meat wasn't kosher, it didn't count. If he ate anything with the meat, say potatoes, it didn't count. A drunkard was someone who drank at least a pint of wine at one sitting. But if the pint of wine was drunk, or the pound of meat was eaten, at a party or during a festival celebration, it didn't count. Moreover, both the meat and wine had to be stolen. If they were given to the son, he was only being polite by eating and drinking the gifts.

But what if a young man stole a pound of kosher meat and a pint of kosher wine, within a few weeks after his Bar Mitzvah, and wolfed them down, separately, without any side dishes, meanwhile cursing his parents? He could be tried by a court; if he was found guilty, he could be sentenced to death. But such a sentence could not be carried out unless both parents gave their permission. Before they could give permission, the parents had to show that they were in perfect health. If they were ill or feeble, they were not considered able to make such a decision.

Under these conditions, no "rebellious" sons suffered the penalty described in the Torah. Yet the rabbis had not changed the Torah, nor added to it, nor subtracted from it.

THE ORDERS OF THE MISHNAH

All these laws, decisions, and rulings are divided in the *Mishnah* into six *Sedarim*, or Orders. Each Order is divided into *Massekhot*, or tractates. In all, there are sixty-three tractates in the *Mishnah*. (A *mishnah* is identified by the name of the tractate, not the order.)

The first order, *Zeraim*, or Seeds, deals with agricultural laws, and also with tithes. A tithe is the portion of a person's income that belongs to the Temple or Temple officials. In ancient days most Jews were farmers or herdsmen, and their tithes were a portion of what they raised; so the link between agricultural law and tithing law is logical. However, the first tractate of this order deals with the rules on prayer. This might not belong logically to Seeds, but opening the *Mishnah* with the rules on prayer seemed a good idea.

The second order, *Moed*, or Festivals, has the laws on observing holidays. The second tractate of this order, called *Erubin*, deals with the boundaries of a man's "place." This belongs here because the laws of the Sabbath say that a man may not walk outside his "place" on the Sabbath. The decisions of the rabbis make it possible to take a long walk on the Sabbath.

The third order, *Nashim*, or Women, deals with marriage, divorce, betrothal, and marriage contracts. The third tractate, *Nedarim*, deals with the rules on vows. This, too, is in its proper place because the vows taken in marriage are among the most important vows.

The fourth order, *Nezikim*, or Damages, includes most decisions in civil and criminal law. The seventh tractate, *Eduyot*, is a collection of odd rulings that didn't seem to fit any place else. And the ninth tractate, *Avoth*, or Sayings of the Fathers, is the most famous of all sections of the *Mishnah*: the *Pirke Avoth*. These are not legal decisions but rules for a good and proper life.

The fifth order, *Kodashim*, or Holy Things, deals with sacrifices and other details of religious practice in the time of the Temple.

The last order, *Tohorot*, or Ritual Cleanness, deals with the ancient laws governing ritual purity.

About half of the *Mishnah* has to do with things that were no longer pertinent when the *Mishnah* was written down, some no longer existed. But they were carefully included, and were as carefully studied and discussed in the schools and study houses of the Jews for almost two thousand years. They are still studied. It isn't the specific facts that are important in these now-irrelevant rules. What is important is the system, the method, the remarkably civilized way in which they were developed.□

STUDY QUESTIONS

1 What is the relationship between the Oral and the Written Law? Is one more important than the other?

2 What historical connection can you see between the beginnings of the Diaspora (define) and the development of the Oral law?

3 Why were the rabbis at first reluctant to have their legal decisions written down?

4 Would it be better if the rulings of the *Mishnah* were simpler and more decisive—that is, a simple yes or a simple no? Why?

5 What is the effect of citing minority, as well as majority, opinions?

6 Are rabbinic interpretations of Scriptural laws a way of changing those laws by reinterpreting them? Did the rabbis of the *Mishnah* think that they were changing tradition?

7 Would it be possible to live with the laws of the Torah today without making any changes at all? Would you feel bound by past decisions and traditions (what lawyers call "precedent")?

8 How would *you* describe a rebellious, drunken, and gluttonous son? Would you define "gluttony" as having too many snacks before dinner? Would a rebellious son be one who refused to go to bed before 11:00 p.m. (or simply one who refused to turn off the T.V. before he had seen his favorite shows)? And finally, what would you *do* with this son of yours: Would you whip him, or have him put to death? Of course, today parents cannot (legally) do either of these things, and since that is so, why should we study an article of rabbinic law that is so completely out-of-date? What can we hope to learn from it?

9 What would happen if, instead of adapting the laws of the Torah and the *Mishnah* to changing circumstances, we decided to forget all about the past and start all over again, creating whatever laws we thought appropriate for the present? Could we call this new system of laws and values "Judaism"?

FOR DISCUSSION

Take the following piece of Torah legislation and consider what the effect would be if these commandments were implemented today. Think about how our society —and specifically our property laws and ways of doing business—would have to change to accommodate Biblical law. Do you really think it could?

[LEV. 25:1-12] The Lord spoke to Moses on Mount Sinai: Speak to the Israelite people and say to them:

When you enter the land that I give you, the land shall observe a sabbath of the Lord. Six years you may sow your field and six years you may prune your vineyard and gather in the yield. But in the seventh year the land shall have a sabbath of complete rest, a sabbath of the Lord: you shall not sow your field or prune your vineyard. You shall not reap the aftergrowth of your harvest or gather the grapes of your untrimmed vines; it shall be a year of complete rest for the land. But you may eat whatever the land during its sabbath will produce. . . .

You shall count off seven weeks of years—seven times seven years—so that the period of seven weeks of years gives you a total of forty-nine years. Then you shall sound the horn loud: in the seventh month, on the tenth day of the month—the Day of Atonement—you shall have the horn sounded throughout the land and you shall hallow the fiftieth year. You shall proclaim release throughout the land for all its inhabitants. It shall be a jubilee for you: each of you shall return to his holding and each of you shall return to his family. That fiftieth year shall be a jubilee for you: you shall not sow, neither shall you reap the aftergrowth or harvest the untrimmed vines.

ABOTH 1 אבות

(This is how the Oral Law was handed down. Moses received the Law from Sinai and committed it to Joshua, who handed it on to the Elders and the Elders to the Prophets . . .)

The Prophets said: Be deliberate in judgment, raise up many disciples, and make a fence around the Law.

Simeon the Just said: By three things is the world sustained: by the Law, by the service, and by deeds of loving-kindness.

Antigonus of Soko received the Law from Simeon; he said: Be not like slaves that do what is ordered by the master only for the sake of receiving a bounty . . .

Jose ben Joezer received the Law from Antigonus; he said: Let thy house be a meetinghouse for the Sages and sit amid them in the dust and drink in their words with thirst.

Jose ben Johanon said: Let your house be opened wide and let the needy be members of your household . . .

Joshua ben Perahyah said: . . . When you judge any man incline the balance in his favor.

Nittai the Arbelite said: Keep far from evil neighbors and do not mix with the wicked . . .

Judah ben Tabbai said: Make not yourself like them that would influence the judges . . .

Simeon ben Shetah said: Examine the witnesses carefully and be cautious in your words lest they (the witnesses) learn from your words to swear falsely.

Shemaiah said: Love labor and hate mastery and seek not acquaintance with the ruling power.

Abtalion said: Ye Sages, give heed to your words . . .

Hillel said: Be of the disciples of Aaron, loving peace and pursuing peace, loving mankind and bringing them close to the Law.

Hillel said: If I am not for myself, who is for me? and being for myself only, what am I? and if not now, when?

Shammai said: Make the study of the Law a fixed habit; say little and do much, and receive all men with a cheerful face.

Rabban Gamliel said: Provide yourself with a teacher and remove yourself from doubt . . .

Simeon ben Gamaliel said: I have grown up among the Sages and I have found nothing better for a man than silence; not the expounding of the Law is the chief thing but the doing of it . . .

Rabban Simeon said: By three things is the world sustained: by truth, by judgment, and by peace, as it is written: "Execute the judgment of truth and peace" [ZECH. 8:16].

THE ORAL TORAH IS THE authoritative interpretation of the Written Torah. This means that the Oral Law must have come from the same Divine Source as the Torah itself. That's why, in the *Mishnah*—which is the written form of the Oral Law—the rabbis gave us its genealogy; they told us how it was handed down. They described how Moses got it from God, and then, how it was transmitted to the scholars who wrote it down in the *Mishnah*.

The *mishnah Aboth 1* begins: "Moses received the (Oral) Torah from Sinai . . ." Since it was at Sinai that he received the Written Torah, the two—Oral and Written Torahs—must be equally sacred. Then the *mishnah* records every individual, group, and pair of sages who inherited the Oral Law from the previous generation and passed it on to the next.

But it's not enough to know who the transmitters were, we have to trust them to pass the Oral Law on exactly as they received it. We have to be sure of their qualifications. The first thousand years or so of this transmission belt are given in the first sentence of the *mishnah*. This covers the period from Moses to the Men of the Great Synagogue. All Jews knew of Moses, Joshua, the Elders, and the Prophets. Their stories are in Scripture and there could be no doubts about them. But begining with the Men of the Great Synagogue, the Jews were divided politically and religiously between the Pharisees and the Sadducees; so from that point on, each person involved transmitting the Oral Law is named.

We do not know exactly who the Men of the Great Synagogue were. (They were also referred to as the Great Assembly or the Great Sanhedrin.) We do not even know whether there was a formal body of that name. But there was, undoubtedly, some body of scholars and judges that had authority in Israel after the return from Babylon in the fifth century BCE. These Men of the Great Synagogue were probably followers of Ezra the Scribe who returned from Babylonian captivity about 450 BCE. From whom did Ezra get the Oral Law? Well, probably from the prophet Ezekiel who preached in Babylon during the captivity.

Beginning with Simeon the Just, who probably lived about 300 BCE, the receivers and transmitters of the Oral Law are identified by name. From Jose ben Joezer and Jose ben Johanon, to Hillel and Shammai, a period of about three hundred years, the receivers are listed in pairs, called *zugot* in Hebrew. According to tradition, the first name in each pair was the *nasi*, the elected head of the Sanhedrin at the time; the second name in the pair was the *ab bet din*, the vice-president of the Sanhedrin who served as the head of the court. It may be that during this troubled period—which included the revolt against the Syrians, the Hasmonean period, and the time of the Romans—the political situation required the guarantee of two names as transmitters rather than one.

For each of the groups and people mentioned in the genealogy of the Oral Law, the compilers of the *Mishnah* added a sentence or two about the scholars' teachings.□

STUDY QUESTIONS

1 Why did the rabbis of the *Mishnah* think it necessary to trace the transmission of the Law back to Moses?

2 What is the "fence" the rabbis speak of? And how can that "fence" be placed "around the Law"? Does this statement really mean that we should:
a protect the laws of the Torah from being changed arbitrarily in every generation?
b or create *additional* laws that will protect and reinforce the original Torah commandment?

Can you think of any other way of interpreting this statement?

3 What does Rabbi Antigonus mean when he teaches: "Be not like slaves that do what is ordered by the master . . ."

4 Why does Shemaiah warn his pupils not to seek the acquaintance of men in power? Who actually ruled Judea during Shemaiah's lifetime (first century BCE)? And how does that help to explain the meaning of Shemaiah's advice?

Do you think Shemaiah's warning has any relevance today—particularly in a democratic society where the "rulers" are representatives of the people?

5 When you first read them, the statements of rabbis Joshua ben Perahyah, Nittai the Arbelite, Judah ben Tabbai, and Simeon ben Shetah seem unrelated; but when you read them more carefully, you see that they are all concerned with securing justice in a just society. How do these rabbis suggest we do that?

6 What is Hillel really saying when he observes: "If I am not for myself, who is for me?" And how do the two questions that follow this one qualify it?

7 Most of us indulge in small talk in the course of a day. Is it to warn us against such trivial speech that Rabbi Simeon ben Gamaliel praises "silence," or is there some other reason for his statement?

Can you perform a mitzvah while talking about it? Or are you more likely to talk about it, rather than *do* it?

8 Many of the rabbis recorded in *mishnah Aboth* say that three "things" are necessary to sustain the world. Of course, the rabbis who said this are seldom in complete agreement on *what* three "things," or virtues are indispensible to mankind. Most likely, they used this device of listing things in threes as a *mnemonic* device (a way of aiding a pupil's memory). But if you had to devise a list of your own, which three virtues or ideals would you single out as *the* most important to people living today?

SANHEDRIN 4 סנהדרין

MISHNAH 1 Non-capital cases (property cases and those for which the penalty is less than death) and capital cases are alike in investigation and examination, for it is written: "Ye shall have one manner of law" [LEV. 24:22]. How do non-capital and capital cases differ?

Non-capital cases are decided by a court of three judges and capital cases are decided by a court of twenty-three.

Non-capital cases can begin with either the arguments for acquittal or for conviction, but capital cases must begin with the reasons for acquittal and may not begin with arguments for conviction.

In non-capital cases the court may reach a decision for either acquittal or conviction by a majority of one; but in capital cases they may reach a verdict of acquittal by a majority of one but a verdict of conviction requires a majority of two.

In non-capital cases the court may reverse its verdict whether it was for acquittal or conviction; but in capital cases they may reverse a verdict of conviction but cannot reverse a verdict of acquittal . . .

In non-capital cases the verdict for conviction or acquittal may be reached the same day (as the trial); in capital cases a verdict of acquittal may be reached the same day, but a verdict of conviction cannot be given until the next day. Therefore trials may not be held on the eve of the Sabbath or a holiday.

MISHNAH 2 In non-capital cases the individual judges give their verdict beginning with the eldest judge (who speaks first), but in capital cases, the judges begin to speak with the youngest.

FROM THE EARLY PAGES OF Genesis through the books of the Prophets, Scripture insists on justice. In Genesis, God calls upon Abraham to command "his children and his household after him, that they ... do righteousness and justice" [GEN. 18:19]. And the prophet Ezekiel's vision of the Holy City, includes this requirement upon the princes of Israel—meaning Israel's government and leaders: "remove violence and spoil, and execute righteousness and justice" [EZ. 45:19].

This constant pairing of righteousness and justice is not merely for literary effect. For Jews, these two qualities have to go together. Justice without righteous-

ness, or righteousness without justice for that matter, can have harsh consequences. The teaching is "there is no true justice unless mercy (righteousness) is part of it" [ZOHAR 4:146b].

The legal system of the Jews described in the *Mishnah* is set up to make sure that no injustice is allowed to sneak into the system and that mercy is given a chance.

The legal system in the Oral Law includes three types of courts: courts of three judges which had jurisdiction over civil cases and divorce (stealing and robbery without violence were considered civil cases); courts of twenty-three judges which dealt with appeals and crimes of violence; and a supreme court of seventy-one judges called the Sanhedrin. Within each type of court there were exact rules of evidence and judgment. The *mishnah Sanhedrin 4* gives some of these rules.

The rules of evidence and procedure in criminal cases were weighted against a conviction because the punishment was irrevocable. In a civil case an error in judgment could be reversed by the payment of money. However, in a capital case a guilty verdict resulted in death — an irreversible verdict. (In those days there were no jails; someone found guilty of murder was punished by whipping or death.)

To lessen the chances of error in judgment, such capital cases had to be tried by a court of twenty-three judges. The arguments for the defense and the arguments for acquittal had to be given first, before the arguments of the prosecution, while the minds of the judges were still fresh and before they had heard the gory claims of the prosecution.

To make certain that transient passions and the prosecution's gruesome dence didn't sway the judges, they were required to sleep on the matter before they could issue a judgment of guilty. Moreover, a judgment of guilty had to be voted by a majority of two or more. That is, at least thirteen of the twenty-three judges had to be sure in their own minds of the accused's guilt.

In a rule written into the Oral Law more than a thousand years before the rule against double jeopardy became part of British common law, the Jewish legal system said that while a judgment for conviction could be reversed, a judgment for acquittal could not be touched.

Unlike the United States Supreme Court, the Jewish judges did not meet before the vote to argue the case among themselves. Each judge made up his own mind, basing his decision solely on his own understanding of the evidence and the Law. The judges learned the views of other court members when the vote was taken and that was done in open court. To make sure that younger judges would not be influenced by the decisions of their older and more experienced colleagues, the youngest judge gave his opinion first, then the next youngest and so on up to the most senior judge.□

STUDY QUESTIONS

1 What is the difference between a capital and a non-capital crime?

2 Why is the court for capital cases larger than the court for non-capital cases? Why do the judges in a capital case deliberate longer?

3 According to Mishnaic law, arguments in a capital case must begin with an argument for acquittal. This procedure gives a certain advantage to the defendant, because it allows his lawyers to present their case first and make the first impression on the judges.

Why did the rabbis insist on this procedure? Why should the defendant in a capital case be given any advantage at all? Shouldn't courts be more concerned about punishing the guilty party than in protecting defendants' rights?

4 In modern American law a defendant is assumed to be innocent until proven guilty. Is that also true of Mishnaic law?

5 How much difference can it make whether a judgment is reached by a majority of one or a majority of two? Why should *mishnah Sanhedrin* insist on a majority of two in capital cases?

Why not make conviction dependent upon a *unanimous* decision of the judges?

6 What does the term "double-jeopardy" mean; why is it unlawful in most systems of law to place someone in "double jeopardy"?

What is the difference between trying someone again who has already been convicted, and trying someone again who had earlier been acquitted? Aren't both cases part of the same legal process?

7 How long are judges (or in our system, juries) allowed to deliberate nowadays? Is there any set time in which a verdict must be reached, or can they (theoretically) deliberate forever?

What happens when a judge or jury cannot reach a verdict? Does the defendant go free, or is he tried again?

FOR DISCUSSION

Consider the following passages from the Torah:

[NUMBERS 35:30] The homicide shall be put to death only on the testimony of witnesses; the testimony of a single witness shall not be enough to bring him to his death.

[DEUTERONOMY 25:1-3] When two men go to law and present themselves for judgment, the judges shall try the case; they shall acquit the innocent and condemn the guilty. If the guilty man is sentenced to be flogged, the judge shall cause him to lie down and be beaten in his presence; the number of the strokes shall correspond to the gravity of the offence. They may give him forty strokes, but not more; otherwise, if they go further and exceed this number, your fellow-countryman will have been publicly degraded.

How does *mishnah Sanhedrin* attempt to capture the *spirit* (as well as reproduce the letter) of this kind of Torah legislation? Does the *Mishnah* go further than the Torah in attempting to assure that a defendant will receive a fair trial and reasonable punishment? Or does the *Mishnah* simply *adapt* the rules of the Torah to a later time?

Why are both the Torah and the *Mishnah* so determined to limit the powers of judges and courts by spelling out exactly how and under what conditions accused persons are to be tried? Do you know of any societies today where the powers of a judge are *unlimited*? What would it be like to live in that society?

PEAH 1 פאה

MISHNAH 2   *Peah* (corners left for the poor) should be not less than one-sixtieth of the harvest. And although they have said that no measure is prescribed for *Peah,* it should ever accord with the size of the field and the number of the poor and the yield of the harvest.

MISHNAH 4   A general rule they have enjoined concerning *Peah*: whatsoever is used for food and is kept watch over (is on private property) and grows from the soil and is all reaped together and is brought in for storage is liable to the law of *Peah*. Grain and pulse (peas, beans, etc.) come within this rule.

MISHNAH 5   Among trees, the sumach, carob, walnut trees, almond trees, vines, pomegranate trees, olive trees and palm trees are subject to the law of *Peah*.

THE *MISHNAH PEAH 1* shows clearly and simply why the Oral Law was necessary if the Jews were to continue to follow the laws given them in Torah. Torah commanded: "And when you reap the harvest of your land, you shall not wholly reap the corner of your field ..." [LEV. 19:9]. This commandment was repeated a few pages further on [LEV. 23:22] with the reason for the commandment added: "...you shall leave them for the poor, and for the stranger." But left the way it was stated in the Torah, the commandment was really no more than a pious wish. A stingy person might leave only a couple of inches in the corners of his field and say that he had fulfilled the commandment. The Oral Law, however, defined those "corners."

The *mishnah* says that corners cannot be less than one-sixtieth of the harvest. Not one-sixtieth of the area, which would seem the most likely measure since the commandment speaks of fields, but one-sixtieth of the weight or measure of the crops taken from that field. The rabbis knew well that the thickest growth is generally in the middle of the field and the thinnest is toward the edges. One-sixtieth of the area at the corners would yield much less corn than one-sixtieth of the entire crop.

Nor did the rabbis say exactly how big the corners should be, that is, how much of the harvest should be given to the poor and the stranger. It would depend, they said, on how big your field was, how good the harvest was, and on how many poor had to be fed. But they did set a minimum: one bushel of corn or peas out of every sixty.

Having settled the question of the minimum size of the corners, the compilers of this *mishnah* addressed the question of what kinds of harvests are included. Being practical people, the rabbis limited the law of *Peah* to things grown for food; it didn't make sense to require a florist to save part of his crop of roses for the poor. It might help the spirits of the hungry, but it wouldn't fill their bellies. Nor did it make sense to require a "corner" of a portion of food taken in the wild, that is, on unowned property. If you gathered huckleberries in the woods, how would you know whether you had left the "corners" of the wood unpicked?

Other than these exceptions, practically everything sown and harvested, or cultivated and harvested, was included in the rule of *Peah*. Some species of grains, vegetables, and fruits were mentioned but this list served only as illustration. It did not mean that crops not listed were excluded. If pomegranates were included, then apples and pears were too.

The *mishnah* on corners did not limit how much could be given to the poor and to strangers. But the keepers of the law knew that the foolish had to be restrained as well as the stingy. Elsewhere there is a rule that you cannot give so much to charity that you beggar your own family. It makes little sense to take the food out of your own children's mouths to feed the children of others.□

STUDY QUESTIONS

1 Why did the rabbis think it necessary to establish a *minimum* amount of harvested grain and produce for the poor? Why is it necessary to enumerate even the varieties of trees that are included within this law?

2 What is the minimum portion to be set aside for the poor? Does *mishnah Peah* permit farmers to set aside *more* than the minimum?

3 Why didn't the rabbis just order landowners to give up some portion of their land to the poor, instead of simply asking them to share some of their food?

4 Have you ever given something you owned and valued to someone who was poor?

5 Should charity of the kind described in this *mishnah* be limited to doles of grain or food? Are there other ways of dealing with poverty or of helping the poor?

6 Many modern social reformers have struggled to resolve the problem of poverty. Every year Congress debates the issues of welfare and unemployment. How does *mishnah Peah* teach us to deal with these problems?

7 What portion of your family's income is set aside for helping the poor? Is it a fixed amount or does it vary from year to year? Is it larger or smaller than the one-sixtieth of a harvest that *mishnah Peah* speaks of?

8 Why is the word for charity in Hebrew (tzedakah) also the word for justice?

FOR DISCUSSION

Mishnah Peah obviously reflects a time when most Jews lived "on the land," or at least in societies that were basically agrarian (the largest and most important industry was agriculture). Today, however, most Jews live in urban, industrial societies, and as a result have very little contact with farms and fields.

How, then, can we be expected to observe this rule of charity?

How would you adapt the underlying principles of this *mishnah* to the realities of modern Jewish life?

BABA METZIA 5 בבא מציעא

MISHNAH 4 No one may provide a shopkeeper with goods to sell under an agreement to take half the profit; no one may give a shopkeeper money to buy produce under an agreement to take half the profits, unless the shopkeeper is paid his wages as a laborer (out of the profits before division). No one may put his eggs to hatch under another man's hens under conditions of sharing the profits, or give his calves or foals to another to rear under the condition of sharing the profits, unless the owner (of the hens or feedlots) is paid the wages of a laborer and the cost of food (for the animals out of the profits).

MAKING LAWS AGAINST ROBbery and stealing is easy. You merely say: If you take what doesn't belong to you, you have robbed. Legislating against lying and false witness is a little more difficult but still fairly simple: Truth proves the lie. The most difficult areas in which to make laws are family quarrels and disputes between employer and employee. In family squabbles neither side may be one hundred percent wrong or one hundred percent right. Quite often there is some justice on both sides. And in the boss-worker relationship, trust, fairness, or how things seem, are often as important as cold facts. Yet we cannot legislate trust and fairness and suchlike qualities. But it is differences in this area—the relationships of the hired and the hirers, between rich and poor, between owners and users—that affect most people most directly and offer the widest possibility for injustice and unrighteousness.

Despite the difficulty with such problems the Jewish legal system tries to govern the relations between those who own and those who work, those who sell and those who buy. The *mishnah Baba Metzia 5* is a portion of that legislation. It deals with what in modern times is called selling on commision or sharecropping.

Behind these laws is the Jewish idea that work is necessary, that work is noble, even holy. Work is both a requirement and a gift from God. The rabbis interpreted, "the Lord God took man and put him in the Garden of Eden to till it and keep it" [GEN. 2:15], to mean that even Adam could not eat until he had worked. They pointed out that even God labored: "He rested from all His work which He had done" [GEN. 11:2].

If work is so important, then the value of work—what we get out of it and what we get from it—is equally important. To deprive a worker of the fruits of his labor is a transgression. The laborer must not be cheated of his pay, neither must he be forced to work for nothing. Most particularly, the worker must not be asked to gamble on his wages.

That is the point of this *mishnah*. The owner of cattle or fowl or land cannot ask the farmer to raise these animals, or work the land, on a gamble. The owner cannot say: If the animals grow well, and the price is right when they are sold, then the worker will be paid. What if the animals die or the price has fallen? Then the worker has labored for nothing. The *mishnah* says: If you want to gamble on the profits, okay, but only after you have paid the laborer his wages.

The same principle holds when the owner of goods, or money, offers them to a storekeeper or salesman who will use his strength, skills, and labor to sell them. Before any division of the profits, you must pay the worker his wages, says this *mishnah*.

In Jewish law, labor has first call upon the proceeds of any venture. Only after the labor has been paid for can the profits be counted. Under the requirement of righteousness, it is assumed that the wages will be fair.□

STUDY QUESTIONS

1 Under what conditions may a businessman *legitimately* profit from his investments?

2 As a general rule, how do the rabbis want people in business to behave?

3 What does it mean to "exploit" someone who works for you? Were the rabbis concerned with the problem of exploitation, and if they were, how can you tell that from this *mishnah*?

Can you identify types of exploitation in contemporary society?

4 If you owned a farm, and you refused to pay your workers any money until all of your crops had been harvested and sold for a profit, would you be violating the spirit of this *mishnah*? Why?

5 Would you be willing to work on a farm (or in an office or a factory) on the *chance* that the goods or services you were producing might just turn out to be profitable? And most importantly, would you be willing to wait to be paid until your employer was absolutely certain that you had earned enough for him?

6 Does this *mishnah* permit a shopkeeper to sell goods "on consignment"? When a shopkeeper offers to sell something on consignment he agrees to display someone else's goods on the chance that his customers might want to buy those goods, but he does not actually pay that "someone" until *after* the goods have been sold—and sold for a profit.

7 You are having a garage sale, and your friend has asked you to include his old bike among the things you are offering for sale. He is willing to wait and see if you are able to sell it, though he does expect that you will sell it for a price large enough to be divided between you, and still make it profitable for you to sell it in the first place. You think his bike is a piece of junk. What should you do?

8 Can you think of *any* type of business venture—searching for oil might be one example—where the merchant or the entrepreneur simply *cannot* guarantee his workers that they will be paid until the venture is successful? Would the rabbis have permitted such ventures in the first place, or would they have exempted exceptionally risky business from this ruling?

24

FOR DISCUSSION

In the Torah we find the following law of wages:

[DEUT. 24:14-15] You shall not keep back the wages of a man who is poor and needy, whether a fellow-countryman or an alien living in your country in one of your settlements. Pay him his wages on the same day before sunset, for he is poor and his heart is set on them: he may appeal to the Lord against you, and you will be guilty of sin.

Mishna Baba Metzia does not, of course, deal with precisely *this* situation, but it does discuss a principle of conduct—ethical behavior—that is directly related to this commandment.

But just what is that principle of conduct? If you had to put it in a literary form like that of the Ten Commandments ("Thou shalt not . . ."), how would you do it? And how would you establish a connection between withholding wages from a poor laborer, and withholding profits from a merchant?

SHEBUOTH 8 שבועות

MISHNAH 1 There are four kinds of guardians: an unpaid guardian, a borrower, a paid guardian, and a hirer. If an animal in the care of an unpaid guardian is lost or damaged, he may take an oath saying that he was not at fault (he did the best he could), and he is free of liability. A borrower must repay the owner no matter the cause of the loss or damage. A paid guardian or hirer may take an oath that he was not at fault if the animal was lamed or driven away or died, but he must repay the owner if the animal was lost or stolen.

THE ORAL LAW DEVELOPED over a period of about six centuries, beginning with the return of the Jews from Babylonian captivity, about 450 BCE, to the end of the last Jewish war against the Romans in 135 CE. (Remember, the *Mishnah* was finally codified about 200 CE.) During these six centuries the great powers of the ancient world were Egypt, Persia, Greece, Syria, and toward the end of the period, Rome. These great powers warred among each other for dominion over that world. Since Israel was the land bridge connecting the home countries of the warring nations, many of these wars were for control of the land of Israel. So, during those six centuries, Jews had to adapt to living under Persian, Egyptian, Greek, Syrian, and Roman rule.

But the land of Israel was not only a route and a battleground for warring armies. It was also the pathway of commerce between East and West, between Europe and Asia and Africa. Israel became a commercial nation as well as a nation of farmers and herdsmen. Its laws, which were eventually collected in the *Mishnah*, had to spell out in great detail the rules governing trade and commerce.

A major source of disputes in business and commerce is who is responsible for goods in the hands of someone other than the owner. An artisan who works on materials left with him for manufacture; a shipmaster who carries cargo belonging to others; a shopkeeper who sells goods belonging to the producer; a banker who takes care of other people's money. And of course, a neighbor who borrows a tool or a piece of furniture.

The *mishnah Shebuoth 8* defines the responsibilites of these various holders of other people's property; in the *Mishnah*, they are called guardians. As was natural for the Jews of that time, the examples were put in terms of cattle, harking back to the time when most Israelites tended flocks—their own and their neighbors'.

The first type of guardian is the unpaid guardian, the neighbor you ask to look after your house while you're away for the weekend. This neighbor is, after all, doing you a favor, so he is not responsible for damage to the house if he takes ordinary care of it. He is not expected to sleep in the house and guard it twenty-four hours a day. If a fire breaks out or thieves enter it in the night, he is not responsible for the loss.

The second type of guardian is the borrower, the neighbor who asks, "Can I use your lawnmower." He is responsible for what he borrows. He is obliged to return the lawnmower (or anything else he borrows) in exactly the same condition it was in when he took it. If he loses it, or breaks it, he must make good the damage.

The third type is the paid guardian, the person to whom you say, "I have to go away on business. I'll give you five dollars a day to watch the house, water the plants, feed and walk the dog." He is responsible for what he is paid to take care of—within limits. He is responsible for damage that could be prevented by watchful care. But if during a windstorm a tree falls on the house, he cannot be asked to pay for the repair. But if he took off for the movies and left the back door open and someone came in and vandalized the house, he is responsible.

The fourth type of guardian is the renter, the person who says, "My car's in the shop; I'll give you so much a day for the use of your car till mine is fixed." Like the paid guardian, he is responsible for proper care of the rented property. If he crashes the car into a tree, he must pay to get the car repaired. But if the car breaks down because of age or improper servicing before the renter took charge, he is not responsible.

From these relatively simple examples, a whole body of case law developed to take care of very intricate commercial dealings. It worked, too, because a thousand years later, in the Middle Ages, the only way an importer in Germany, France, or England could do business with a supplier in Turkey, Egypt, or Arabia was through Jewish middlemen who were bound by Jewish law.□

STUDY QUESTIONS

1 What are the four kinds of guardians identified in this *mishnah*? How do they differ from one another? Do modern systems of law make similar distinctions?

2 We have laws today that establish limits to personal liability, but how do those laws compare to the laws of this *mishnah*? For example, are you responsible for your parents' debts? Could you be sent to jail if *they* went bankrupt?

3 Borrowing is something that normally takes place between neighbors or friends — at least "informal" borrowing does, as opposed to going to the bank for a loan. Why is it necessary to have laws to regulate "informal" loans? Can't friends just resolve whatever problems may arise between them?

Do you know of any cases where neighbors or friends have sued one another over some lost, borrowed article?

4 If you borrowed something valuable from a friend—a stereo, for example, or video games—and lost them, or damaged them beyond repair, would you feel *morally* bound to replace them? Or would you simply apologize for having accidentally destroyed or lost an expensive thing? Would your friend be *satisfied* with just an apology?

5 What would the rabbis have said if a friend gave you his rare tropical fish to look after while he was away on vacation, only to discover, when he returned, that his fish had died because you had not fed them or changed their water? Would the rabbis have held you responsible?

But what if you *had*, in fact, fed them and done everything your friend had asked you to do and they died anyway? Would you have to replace them?

6 Do banks and lending agencies, today, operate on the same legal basis as this *mishnah*? Consider the following situation:

You have just bought a new car, and you have already started making monthly payments on it. One day, quite by accident—and through no fault of yours—your car malfunctions, careens into several parked cars, causing hundreds of dollars in damages. Fortunately no one is hurt, but your car is a total wreck.

Your insurance company will pay you only a percentage of what your car is really worth, and it will cover most (but not all) of the expenses that result from the damage your car has caused. And you now have nothing to drive. The bank insists that you pay off what is left of your loan—even though your car no longer exists.

How would the rabbis have handled this situation? Would they have been able to decide who was the real "guardian" of your car, and who was really liable for all the damage and loss?

FOR DISCUSSION

You are serving as one of the rabbinic judges of a modern *Bet Din*, and you have been asked for a ruling, consistent with the legal principles of *mishnah Shebuoth,* on the following case:

A baby-sitter is popping popcorn one evening on the stove, when she hears one of the children start to scream. She runs out of the kitchen, leaving the stove on, and while she is out of the room the kitchen curtains catch fire. The house begins to burn very quickly, and when she realizes what has happened, she has only enough time to gather up all of the children in the house and escape. The house burns to the ground.

Which of the rules of guardianship applies here? Is the baby-sitter responsible for the children she is guarding or for the house? Or should she be held responsible for both? And can she, as a minor, be expected to make restitution for the family's losses? What would your judgment be?

BABA METZIA 7 בבא מציעא

MISHNAH 4 (A laborer may eat of the fruits among which he labors.) If he worked among figs he may not eat grapes, and if among grapes he may not eat figs; but he may refrain from eating until he reaches the best fruits and then eat. He may eat (of these fruits) only during the time of his labors . . . but they (the Rabbis) had said: Laborers may eat as they go from one furrow to another or as they return from the winepress; and an ass may eat while it is being unloaded.

MISHNAH 5 A laborer may eat cucumbers, even a denar's worth, and dates even a denar's worth. Rabbi Eleazar ben Hisma says: A laborer may not eat more than his wages' worth. But the Sages permit it, yet they would teach a man not to be so greedy as to close the door against himself. (Eat so much that the employer will not hire him again.)

MISHNAH 6 A man may agree to accept extra pay and give up the right to eat of the fruit that he is hired to pick. He may do so for himself, for his son or daughter that are of age, for his bondman or bondwoman that are of age, and for his wife, since they have understanding. But he may not make such an agreement for his son or daughter that are not of age, or for his bondman or bondwoman that are not of age, nor for his beasts, since these have no understanding.

I N THE *MISHNAH BABA Metzia 7* is an example of the sweet reasonableness, the sense of fairness, the exactly right balance between the requirements of justice and righteousness that the rabbis tried to teach. At harvest time, the fruits and vegetables belong to the owner of the orchard and farm. That is justice. But it would be unfair—unrighteous—to deny a taste of these fruits and vegetables to the people who labor all day harvesting them.

Torah says: "You shall not muzzle the ox when he treads out the corn" [DEUT. 25:4]. This commandment says, in effect, it would be cruel to make the ox tread out the grain—that's how grain was threshed in ancient times — without allowing him a sweet mouthful from time to time. In this *mishnah* the rabbis extended the commandment to human harvesters. They also made sure that this compromise between justice and righteousness wasn't twisted by either stingy owners or greedy workers.

To protect the laborers who picked the fruits and vegetables, the Sages said that the pickers couldn't be told to eat only the scrawny, unmarketable apples or figs or whatever. The harvesters could wait until they reached the lushest fruits, then take some. Nor could they be held to the letter of the law and be restricted to eating only while they were actually picking. They were allowed to stick ripe fruit in their pockets, nibbling on it while walking from one row to another; they could eat grapes while walking back from the place to which they had delivered the full hampers.

And to protect the farmer from losing a sizable part of his crops, the pickers were allowed to eat only the produce they were picking. They couldn't wander into the next field to get something more to their liking. Nor could they take a basketful home.

The makers of the *mishnah* were too smart to write into law exactly how much a laborer might eat while working in the fields. What is a nibble to some folks is a meal to others. Some rabbis said a laborer was allowed to eat "even a denar's worth." (A denar bought a lot of vegetables in those times.) Rabbi Eleazar thought a harvester should be restricted to eating no more than his day's wages would buy in the market—which would mean that the total cost to his employer would be twice the actual monetary wages. But the majority of the Sages considering this question refused to put a monetary limit on this nibbling. They merely cautioned workers: Don't be a pig; you'll end up with nothing because the farmer won't hire you the next day.

In section 5 of the *mishnah* the rabbis again showed that beautiful balance between rigid law and understanding of human nature. When the owner of an orchard hired pickers, he generally hired the whole family or household. And if the family needed money desperately, the head of the family could make an agreement with the farmer that no one would eat of the fruit they were picking. Instead, the owner would pay the family an extra amount of money— roughly the value of what they would otherwise have eaten. The head of the family could make this agreement for all members of the household—except for the children and animals. Those members of the household who had reached the age of understanding, say eleven or twelve, could be barred from eating. But, said the Sages, it would be cruel —unrighteous—to make little children and animals spend a day in a vineyard or orchard and deny them a taste of a luscious grape or a sweet fig.□

STUDY QUESTIONS

1 According to *mishnah Baba Metzia*, when *may* a farm worker eat the fruit he is harvesting? Which fruit is he permitted to eat, and how much?

2 Why don't the rabbis attempt to apply these rules to the children of farm workers? Or animals?

3 Why would any farm worker voluntarily give up the right to eat the fruit he was picking? Is it fair to even ask him or to give him that choice?

4 If the rabbis were writing *mishnah Baba Metzia* today, would they have extended the privileges of the farm worker to workers in a canning or packaging factory?

Do you think that worker is entitled to taste the food he is packing? Can you think of any reason why such a worker should never be allowed to taste the food he is wrapping, or canning, or crating?

5 And what about workers in industries that have nothing to do with agriculture? Does a worker, for example, in a computer chip factory have the right to take a calculator he is assembling?

6 How does this *mishnah* express a feeling of compassion for working animals, as well as working humans?

7 *Mishna Baba Metzia* records a difference of opinion between Rabbi Eleazar ben Hisma and his fellow *tannaim* over the question of just how much a farm worker ought to be allowed to eat in the fields. Which of the two positions do you agree with: Should a farm worker be permitted to eat only his wages worth, or should he be permitted to eat as much as he really wants?

8 Today the question of how much and what kinds of fruit a farm worker can eat in the fields would be negotiated by a labor union, but in the period of the *Mishnah* there were no unions of any kind. Consequently, the rabbis had to write legal opinions that would be binding to both parties.

Do you think that modern labor negotiators are as concerned with the welfare of a farm worker's family—and the conditions of labor—as were the rabbis? What evidence can you cite for your opinions?

FOR DISCUSSION

In an earlier passage in *Baba Metzia 7* (one not quoted in your text) the rabbis cite the following law from the Torah:

[DEUT. 23:24] When you go into another man's vineyard, you may eat as many grapes as you wish to satisfy your hunger, but you may not put any into your basket.

Obviously this piece of Torah legislation served the rabbis as a kind of precedent—that is, an earlier instance of the type of ruling they were trying to formulate themselves, centuries later. But what exactly does the original Torah statement say? Does the Torah actually set limits on the amount of fruit that can be consumed by farm or vineyard workers, or does it simply prevent those workers from carrying off the whole of a farmer's crop? What do you think is the real intent of the Torah? Why should it matter, for example, whether a farm worker eats a dozen pieces of fruit in the fields, or carries the same dozen pieces of fruit off in a basket?

How would you have clarified the Torah law to avoid this confusion?

BABA BATHRA 2 בבא בתרא

MISHNAH 1   None may dig a cistern near his fellow's cistern; nor may he dig a trench, vault, water-channel, or washing pool closer than three-handsbreadths away from his fellow's wall; and he must plaster the wall with lime. Piles of olive-refuse, manure, salt, lime or stones may not be kept closer than three-handsbreadths from his fellow's wall; and he must plaster the wall with lime. Seeds or a plough may not be kept closer than three handsbreadths from the wall . . .

THE AMERICAN POET ROBert Frost wrote: "Good fences make good neighbors." The ancient Jews knew well that a good fence between neighbors lessens the chances for disputes, so fences were required. Moreover, to lessen even further the possibility of quarrels between neighbors, Jewish law went a step beyond Robert Frost's advice.

By the rules in the *mishnah Baba Bathra 2*, a good neighbor does not dig right alongside a fence or wall because this might undermine the fence. And any water in the digging might run into the neighbor's yard.

However, if you must dig a water channel, a trench, or a pit, you do so at least three handsbreadths away from the fence — that's about twelve inches. And to make sure that even such holes or trenches are no threat to the fence or to the neighbor's land, you must plaster the wall.

Water and undermining are not the only hazards a good neighbor must guard against. Things that might rot — the *mishnah* gives olive pits and manure as examples — must also be kept at least twelve inches away from the fence, which must be plastered. It is the same with chemicals — salt and lime, for example — which might destroy the wall.

The rules in this *mishnah* do not deal with major problems, with large sums of money or international trade. They deal with small everyday problems. But these are just as important because many more people have fences — and the possibility of disputes over fences — than have the problems of high finance.

As much as anything else, the purpose of the *Mishnah* is to preserve *shalom bayit*, peace in the house. Not just the individual house but the house of Israel.☐

BABA BATHRA 2 בבא בתרא

MISHNAH 3 No one may open a baker's shop or a dyer's shop under his fellow's storehouse, nor may he keep a cattle-stall nearby. They (the Sages) have allowed a baker's shop and a dyer's shop under a winestore, but not a cattle-stall. (Because it was thought that warmth improves the wine but the smell of cattle would spoil it.) A man may protest against a shop within a courtyard and say to the shopkeeper, "I cannot sleep because of the noise of those who go in and out." He that makes utensils should go to the market to sell. But no one may protest to another and say, "I cannot sleep because of the noise of the hammer, or because of the millstones, or because of the noise of children."

THE THIRD SECTION OF *Baba Bathra 2* continues the rules aimed at preserving *shalom bayit*. This time it deals with the problem of noise, and smell, and possible interference with your neighbor's livelihood.

In order to understand this *mishnah* you have to imagine the life-style of a town or city in ancient Judea. The building is two or three stories high, roughly U-shaped, with a large courtyard in the open part of the U. The building is divided into five, six, or eight separate units, each unit a combination of dwelling and shop. The people who live in this sort of ancient condominium not only eat and sleep there, they also have their workshops there. The shops are on the ground floor, the storehouses and dwelling places upstairs.

Seven or eight families living close together around a common courtyard would in itself raise the possibility of frequent quarrels. Add their workshops, and the possibilities are multiplied. So careful rules were laid down in order to maintain not only peace, but justice.

As a general rule says the *mishnah Baba Bathra 2:3*, you cannot put a bakery or a dye shop under another person's dwelling or storeroom. The heat from the bakery ovens and the heat and smell from the dye vats will bother the people above and might spoil their goods. And you can't keep cows nearby either, for obvious reasons. The rabbis did make one exception: If you keep wine in your upstairs storeroom, someone may put a bakery or dye shop underneath the winestore because the heat will help rather than hurt the wine.

Next the *mishnah* deals with the question of noise. The Sages differentiated between the noise created by a workman plying his trade and the noise of buying and selling what he made. The noise of tools, "of a hammer or ... millstones," are a necessary part of making a living. This noise has to be accepted because it cannot be transferred. But the noise of buying and selling can be transferred to the marketplace, so that clamor need not be accepted. An artisan can work at his dwelling place; but he has no right to sell his wares there if his neighbors object.

There's a note added to this *mishnah*: "No one may protest ... because of the noise of children." It seems unnecessary. If people live around a common courtyard, and there are children, there's bound to be noise. But for the legalists who might ask, "Where does it say that children are allowed to disturb my peace?" the Sages added the note to *Baba Bathra 2:3*—for the sake of *shalom bayit*.□

36

STUDY QUESTIONS

1 What does *shalom bayit* mean? Why is it so important a principle that several *mishnayot* try to embody it in specific laws?

2 How do we protect an individual's property rights nowadays? Do you think individual rights are more or less important than the rights of the community—and especially when the two are in conflict?

Consider the case of a proposed highway which the state wants to construct through your backyard. Should you, the individual property owner, have the right to veto this construction, or should you sacrifice your rights for the good of the community?

3 How far should anyone be prepared to go to prevent the possibility of a quarrel with a neighbor?

Take, for example, the case of a neighbor who has an allergy to rosebushes. Would it be reasonable of him to demand that you cut down all of your rosebushes just because they make him sneeze?

Or what about the neighbor who objects to children playing in the street because they make too much noise? Should you keep your children inside to avoid offending your neighbor? Should you move? Or should you simply conclude that your neighbor is cranky and ignore him altogether?

4 Have you ever seen a sign hanging outside an apartment building that reads: "Adults only—no children or pets"? How would the rabbis who wrote *mishnah Baba Bathra* have reacted to his sign?

5 Let us assume that you strike oil on your property one day, and that you want to begin pumping it commercially. The only way that you can do this, however, is if you set up an enormous oil rig that will extend well beyond your boundary line. Furthermore, you know perfectly well that once the drilling starts, some of the oil will spill over onto your neighbor's property. What should you do?

6 If you raked up the leaves on your front lawn and then, accidentally, dumped them so close to your neighbor's driveway that it became almost impossible for him to pull his car out, would the rabbis have concluded that you were at fault? Why?

7 How can the principle of *shalom bayit* be extended to the world of international diplomacy? Should neighboring countries be expected to maintain "good fences" and avoid infringing on each other's rights? Just how can that be done?

8 Today, most industrialized nations have become very concerned with the problems of industrial waste and environmental pollution. Everyone, of course, would like to have clean air and water, but often no one can agree on who is ultimately responsible for cleaning up a problem that already exists, or exactly how to prevent one from developing in the future.

How might the principle of *shalom bayit* apply to situations like this? Consider the following case study:

A petroleum refinery has just been constructed in your neighborhood, and already it has started to emit foul odors. However, this refinery also provides jobs for several thousand neighbors, and it also contributes significantly to the county's tax base (increasing the amount of money available for hospitals, schools, and other social services). Furthermore, the oil and the gas it produces are needed by the community. What are you to do?

FOR DISCUSSION

You have just been elected to your city council and given the responsibility of redrawing city ordinances affecting property rights and zoning privileges. Which rights would you be careful to safeguard, and which privileges would you try to restrict?

Would you, for example, allow a city dump to be built in the middle of a residential neighborhood?

BABA BATHRA 9 בבא בתרא

MISHNAH 1 If a man died and left sons and daughters, and the property was great, the sons inherit and the daughters receive maintenance; but if the property was small the daughters receive maintenance and the sons go a-begging. Admon says: The sons may say, "Must I suffer because I am a male?" Rabban Gamaliel said: I approve of the words of Admon.

THIS *MISHNAH* CAME INTO being about two thousand years ago, so it is a mistake to apply today's ideas about equality of the sexes to its rules. It is a fact of history that in ancient times women were not treated equally with men. To argue about this is as silly as asking why Columbus didn't use a steamboat rather than wasting all those months at sea. Social and legal improvements develop even more slowly than scientific ones.

Despite this lag in ideas about equality, Jewish law did provide protections for women that were quite advanced for those times. Among these protections was the right of daughters to inherit their father's estate if there were no sons. And even if there were sons to inherit, the daughters had to be provided for. They had to be taken care of by their brothers out of the inherited money. If there was not enough money in the estate to take care of the daughters and give something to the sons, the daughters' needs came first. Only after the women were taken care of could the brothers take from the estate.

Nor was the daughters' upkeep the only claim they had on the inheritance left by the father. The sons also had to provide dowries for their sisters. The idea of a dowry—the money or goods that a wife brings to her husband—may also be displeasing to us today, but it was a necessity in marriages in those days. The sons had to give their sisters dowries as well as maintenance until they got married.

How much did the brothers give as dowry out of the father's estate? Theoretically, they were supposed to poll their father's friends and get an idea of how much he would have given. But this was a chancy proposition. In general, ten percent of the estate was considered a respectable dowry—as long as there weren't too many daughters.□

STUDY QUESTIONS

1 According to *mishnah Baba Bathra,* when a man leaves only a small amount of property to his children, who has the *first* claim upon the money: the daughters or the sons?

Does that seem fair?

2 Why did the rabbis insist that sons must provide "maintenance" and dowries for the daughters of the family?

3 Had you been born during Mishnaic times, how important do you think inheritance money would have been to you—especially if you were a woman?

4 Would you have tried to change this law had you been Rabban Gamaliel? And if you would have, how would you have changed it?

Would you, for example, have freed the sons of the family from any obligation towards the daughters? Or would you have insisted that an equal share of the father's inheritance go to every child, irrespective of sex?

5 Why didn't it ever occur to the rabbis to require that the daughters provide for the sons, even if they were married?

Wouldn't that be as fair a procedure as the reverse?

6 In what ways does this *mishnah* reveal the great importance that rabbinic Judaism always placed on family life, and on the responsibility of family members for each other?

FOR DISCUSSION

Consider a more modern situation. Take a family of three children: two brothers (aged twenty and eighteen) and a sister (aged fifteen). Both of their parents have just been tragically killed in an automobile accident, and the young people are now left with relatively little money and a pile of unpaid bills and debts.

After adding up all of their resources, the brothers discover that there is just enough money left over to send one of them to college—and only one! What should they do?

44

BABA KAMMA 8 בבא קמא

MISHNAH 6 If a man cuffed his fellow, he must pay him four zuz. Rabbi Judah says in the name of Rabbi Jose the Galilean: one hundred zuz. If he slapped him, he must pay 200 zuz. If he struck him with the back of his hand, he must pay him 400 zuz. . . . This is the general rule: all is in accordance with a persons's honor. . . .

MISHNAH 7 Even though a man pays the person who suffered the indignity, the action is not forgiven until he asks forgiveness from the person offended. If the offended person does not forgive the person who asks forgiveness, he is called merciless. Where do we learn this: Because it is written: "And Abraham prayed to God and God healed Abimelech" [GEN. 20:17].

If a man said, "blind my eye," or "cut off my hand," or "break my foot," he that does so shall be guilty. This is so even if the person asking for the injury says he will not hold the injurer guilty. If a man says, "break my jug," or "tear my garment," he that does so is guilty. However, if a man says, "tear my garment," or "break my jug and you will not be culpable," then he who does so is not guilty. However, if a man says, "do such and such to so and so (to another person), then the person who does the injury is guilty regardless of anything said.

FROM THE MOST ANCIENT courts to today's, halls of justice have been crowded with cases in which money damages are asked because one person inflicted hurt and pain upon another. Someone slips on an icy walk; he sues the householder. Someone is hit by a car; the victim sues the owner of the car. The victim asks for money to pay the medical bills; he asks for money to make up for the wages he lost while recovering; and in most cases the victim also asks for money to pay for his pain and suffering, even for his "mental anguish."

How much is pain worth? Physical pain or mental pain? How do you measure pain in terms of dollars? Does a punch in the belly hurt more than a kick in the shins?

In the *mishnah Baba Kamma 8*, the rabbis accepted the decisions of Rabbi Judah, who repeated a decision given by Rabbi Jose. Rabbi Judah said, in effect, that a court cannot measure the degree of pain suffered by another. Nor is pain the most important thing. More important than the pain is the affront, the indignity, the possible loss of respect that might follow when one person hits another.

Pain is known only to the victim and cannot be weighed or measured. What we must consider is the insult, which depends on how and when and where the pain was inflicted. If one person cuffs another—gives him a push or a punch—the penalty is one hundred zuz (about twenty-five dollars today, but a large sum two thousand years ago). However, if he slapped him in the face, a degrading act, the slapper must pay two hundred zuz. The penalty is doubled even if the slap didn't hurt as much as the cuff. And if he slapped him with the back of his hand—a very insulting act back then—the penalty was four hundred zuz. About one hundred dollars, a great sum in those days).

It is not the pain that counts, says Rabbi Judah, but the loss of a person's dignity or sense of honor. That is the standard by which hurts to the person, hurts to his reputation, hurts to the sense of self, should be measured by a court.

But hurting someone is also a transgression, a violation of God's law which Hillel shortened to: Do not do to others what is hateful to you. Such a transgression cannot be wiped out merely by paying money. If it could, a rich man could go around town slapping anyone who displeased him and get away with it by paying what to a rich man was very little. Transgressions against another human being can only be forgiven by asking the victim's forgiveness. The aggressor must go to the person he affronted and say: "I am sorry. Will you forgive me?"

If such an apology is made honestly, without reservation, it must be accepted by the victim. If he doesn't, the community will reject him as merciless.

Then the rabbis turned to a more shadowy area. What if someone asks another to hurt him—say, to break his leg, or, more likely, to blacken his eye and bloody his nose. There are such instances. Even if the one asking to be hurt says that he will not hold you responsible, it is absolutely forbidden. The Law does not permit one person to harm another except in war or as the order of a lawful court.

This absolute rule covers only living beings. It does not extend to things. If someone says, "My zipper is stuck hard, cut me out of this jacket," you may do so as long as the owner of the jacket agrees that you will not be responsible. If someone asks you to break through the back door of his house because he's locked out and must get in, you may do so as long as he absolves you of responsibility for the damage.□

STUDY QUESTIONS

1 What has Hillel's statement—"Do not do to others what is hateful to you"—to do with the legal penalties the rabbis impose on people who hurt other people?

2 Why do the rabbis attempt to work out a scale of financial compensation for people who have been injured by someone else? Is it possible to put a price tag on an insult or an injury? Or are such penalties intended as both a punishment and a deterrence to someone who might be tempted to hurt another person?

3 What has personal honor to do with the amount to be paid when someone has been insulted or physically hurt? Can a sense of personal honor be restored? What penalties would you recommend in a case where the injured party was insulted but not physically hurt?

4 Which would you rather do: pay someone you had hurt, or ask his or her forgiveness? Why?

5 Why is it necessary for the injured party to accept the apologies of the person who hurt him? Why do the rabbis insist on this? Shouldn't someone who has been hurt have the right to stay angry at the person who hurt him—whether or not that person asks for forgiveness?

6 On *Yom Kippur* we are instructed to pray to God for forgiveness for all of the ways we have broken His laws; but we are also instructed to ask pardon of our fellow human beings for all of the ways we have injured them.

How does this double idea of repentance relate to *mishnah Baba Kamma* and to the problem of personal injury?

7 Why is it sometimes necessary that people in dangerous occupations—like firemen or policemen—be released from legal responsibility for someone else's property?

Consider the following situation:

A company of firemen are called to put out a fire, but when they arrive on the scene they discover that they can't get their hoses hooked up to the nearest fire pump because someone has parked his car illegally in front of that pump. If they use axes to smash the windows of his car, then release the brakes and move it away, the car's owner may sue them for damages. How would you protect these firemen from liability?

FOR DISCUSSION

Try to imagine yourself in the following situation: You have had a violent quarrel with a close friend. You have insulted each other, and maybe even traded blows. Now you want to "make up," but you're not quite sure how to go about it, and you're not quite sure if your friend wants to make up as much as you do.

What will you do? Your choices might look something like this:

1. You can stay angry and lose your friend for good.
2. You can swallow your pride and ask him or her to forgive you, whether or not you think you're really to blame for the quarrel in the first place.
3. You can ask your friend if he or she is willing to forget all about it, without even mentioning the cause of the quarrel.
4. Or you can try to strike up a conversation with your friend and pretend that nothing ever happened between you.

Which of these alternatives would you prefer? Which alternative seems to be the most practical? And finally, which alternative do you think the rabbis would have urged you to take?

GITTIN 4 גיטין

MISHNAH 6 If a man sold his bondman to a gentile or to anyone outside the Land of Israel, he goes forth a freedman. Captives should not be ransomed for more than their value for the general good (lest kidnapping become a lucrative trade). Captives should not be helped to escape, as a precaution for the general good. (Otherwise captives might be kept in chains.) And none shall buy scrolls, phylacteries, or mezzuzahs from gentiles for more than their value, as a precaution for the common good. (Lest theft of these articles be encouraged.)

SLAVERY WAS A FACT OF life in ancient times. Rebuking the Israelites of two thousand years ago, because they lived as everyone else in the world lived at that time, is pointless. Jews owned slaves then. Jews were slaves then.

However, Jewish slaveholding was very carefully controlled by law. Those laws were, by the standards of those times, quite humane. A Jew who owned slaves owned only their labor; he did not own their bodies. He could not misuse or hurt his slaves; he could not interfere with their marriages or break up their families.

Moreover a Jew who owned a Jewish slave (bondman) did not own him forever. A Jewish slave could be held for only seven years. After seven years the Jewish slave had to be given his freedom. And on release the slave's former owner had to give him sufficient food and goods to last until the freedman could get settled.

That was the law governing Jewish owners of Jewish slaves. But that law was enforceable only in the land of Israel, and only among Jews. So it was forbidden to sell a slave outside of Israel, or to a gentile who would not be bound by Jewish law concerning slaves.

In Jewish law stealing things is a civil crime because it is reversible. That is, if the thing stolen is returned, the damage is made good. So the penalty for stealing property is a monetary penalty. Where the Ten Commandments says, "Thou shalt not steal," the reference is to stealing people—for which the penalty is death. (Jews became slaves to other Jews by voluntarily agreeing to it; in such cases they were called bondmen.) That's why in the *mishnah Gittin 4:6* the rabbis moved naturally from questions of slavery, to captives, to theft of religious articles.

The rulings on captives appear on the surface to be harsh: Don't pay too much ransom; don't help captives escape. But the true purpose of the rulings is to lessen the chances of being taken captive, and to ease the conditions of persons taken captive.

The rabbis said don't pay large ransoms; if there's little profit in it, kidnapping and taking hostages would be a poor business. (Modern Israel refuses to redeem any captives—who are today called hostages.) However, if captives are taken, and the kidnappers think there will be attempts to free them, the captives will be chained up. So don't let the captor think you'll help the captives escape.

Only a *sofer*, a scribe, who must be a pious Jew, may copy the Torah and write the verses that are inside *tefillin* and *mezzuzot*. So these religious articles are not likely to be found in non-Jewish hands. If they are, they were probably stolen. Don't make stealing such articles worthwhile, say the Sages, by ransoming them.□

EDUYOTH 1 עֵדוּיוֹת

MISHNAH 13   If a man was half bondman and half freedman (for example, if he had belonged to two brothers and one brother had freed him), he shall labor one day for his master and another day for himself. So say the School of Hillel. The School of Shammai say: This is good for the master, but what of the man? He cannot marry a free woman and he cannot marry a bondwoman; shall he remain childless? Was not the world created for fruition and increase? For the general good they (the community) should compel his master to set him free, and the bondman writes a bond of indebtedness for half his value. The School of Hillel changed their opinion and taught according to the opinion of the School of Shammai.

FOR A GENERATION, FROM about 10 BCE to about 10 CE, Hillel was the *nasi* or head of the Sanhedrin, and, therefore, head of the Jewish community of Israel. According to the *mishnah Aboth 1* (see page 11), Hillel was one of the two-man combinations, called *zugot* in Hebrew, who transmitted the Oral Law. His colleague was Shammai, the *ab bet din* or vice-president of the Sanhedrin. These two, Hillel and Shammai, were the greatest teachers and masters of the Law in their time.

Both Hillel and Shammai followed the Law exactly in their decisions, but in the delicate balance between justice and righteousness, Hillel's judgments tended to lean more toward righteousness; Shammai's decisions tended to lean more toward justice. It was the same with the followers and disciples who made up the Bet Hillel, the School of Hillel, and the Bet Shammai.

For example, in the case of a woman whose husband had not been heard from for years, Bet Hillel said that the woman could be considered a widow and thus able to remarry as long as there had been a report that the husband was dead. Bet Shammai ruled that a report of the husband's death was not enough; eyewitnesses had to swear to the death. In effect, Shammai said: This is the law; Hillel said: True but for the sake of compassion, let us bend it a little.

And this is how Hillel and Shammai have been viewed traditionally. Hillel was easier, softer, and more inclined to give one the benefit of the doubt. Shammai was stricter, and more demanding that the letter of the Law be followed.

However, as is obvious from the *mishnah Eduyoth 1:13,* they didn't always divide that way. Sometimes Hillel took the harsher line and Shammai the softer. In this *mishnah,* a father has died leaving his property, including a slave, to his two sons. One son immediately gives up his ownership of the slave. He frees his half. But the other brother refuses to follow. This creates confusion about the slave's rights and duties and the case is brought before the *Bet Din.*

Hillel ruled that the half-slave should be free half of the time. That is, he would be a free man on Sundays, Tuesdays, and Thursdays; but he would be a slave on Mondays, Wednesdays, and Fridays. It came out even because by Jewish law even slaves were free from work on the Sabbath.

Shammai, on the other hand, held that while Hillel's decision would be good for the master, it was not so good for the servant. He gave as an example: A slave could not marry a free woman; a free man could not marry a slave. The half-slave was doomed to a half-life if Hillel's decision stood. Shammai ruled that the half-slave should be given his complete freedom and that he give his master—the one who would not free him—a bond for the value of half a slave.

So, in this case, Hillel interpreted the law strictly, without real consideration of the slave's humanity. Shammai took the more humane view. In the end, however, the School of Hillel came to the understanding of the School of Shammai and fulfilled the commandment to judge with justice and righteousness.□

STUDY QUESTIONS

1 How could the Jews of Mishnaic times allow themselves to own slaves? Why didn't the rabbis simply outlaw slavery altogether? Wouldn't that have been a more logical course than attempting to treat slaves more compassionately?

2 What limits did the Torah impose upon the powers of a slaveholder (see DEUT. 15:12-18, for example)? What was a slaveholder not allowed to do?

3 Why does *mishnah Gittin* declare that any slave who is sold to someone living outside of the land of Israel becomes a "freedman"?

4 Why would anyone voluntarily sell himself (or herself) or his children into slavery? What could drive someone to so desperate a decision?

5 *Mishnah Gittin* discusses both the stealing of people (i.e. kidnapping) and the stealing of phylacteries and mezzuzot in the same breath. Does that mean that, in the rabbis' eyes, someone who has been kidnapped or taken captive is no more important than a stolen article? Why are the two cases considered together?

6 Why did the School of Hillel finally come round to the views of the School of Shammai on the question of the half-bondman, half-freedman?

7 Why is it important that a slave be free to marry and produce children?

8 How do you think the rabbis of the *Mishnah* would have dealt with the problem of hostages being held by a band of terrorists? Would they have agreed to ransom payments? Would they even have negotiated with them? Would you?

FOR DISCUSSION

Since we no longer own slaves today, the laws of these segments of the *Mishnah* would certainly appear obsolete. However, people still fall into debt, even today, and creditors (the people to whom money is owed) find themselves facing choices that are remarkably similar to those made centuries ago by slave-holding Jews.

Try to imagine, then, that someone owes you a great deal of money, so much in fact that he cannot even conceive of paying you back in the near future. Instead, he offers to work for you for nothing in order to pay off at least a portion of that debt—thus making himself a "bondsman" in fact if not in name.

What should you do? Should you accept his offer and put him to work doing odd jobs around the house, all day, every day in the week? If he works that much he will never be able to look for or hold down a job, and that means that he will never be in a position to pay you back what he owes you.

Should you, on the other hand, tell him to forget about the debt entirely? That would be unjust to you, since you loaned him a lot of money in good faith—money that you might have spent on yourself and your family.

How would the rabbis have resolved this dilemma?

54

PESAHIM 4 פסחים

MISHNAH 1   Where the custom is to do work until midday on the day before Passover, they may do so; where the custom is not to do work on that day, they may not work. If a man went from a place where work was permitted to a place where it was not permitted, or from a place where it was not to a place where it was, he must follow the strictest rule. But let no man behave differently (than would be acceptable where he now is) lest it lead to conflict.

MISHNAH 4   Where the custom is to eat roast lamb on the nights of Passover, they may eat so; where the custom is not to eat it roasted they may not eat it so. . . .

MISHNAH 5   Where the custom is to do work on the Ninth of Ab, they may do so; where the custom is not to work, they may not work. . . .

EVEN IN THE TIME OF THE Sages of the Mishnah, generally the first and second centuries CE, the Jews were spread over much of the known world. They all followed the same Law but with time and distance many customs changed. Even within the land of Israel the Jews of Tiberias did some things differently from the Jews of Beersheva. The Jews who lived among the Persians for several centuries certainly developed different customs from those who lived in Egypt for seven or eight centuries.

So what does a Babylonian (Persian) Jew do when he goes to study in Jerusalem? Or a Jew of Hebron when he goes to work in Alexandria? The lesson taught by the *mishnah* is: The visitor does not offend his host!

If you're accustomed to working half a day on the day of the *Pesach seder*, but your hosts do not work at all on that day, take a holiday. If your mother said you must eat roast lamb on *Pesach*, but your hosts do not eat lamb, don't ask for lamb. Eat what they give you and say "thank you."

Hillel had said it some time before: What you wouldn't want anyone to do to you, don't do to any fellow creature. Of course, this doesn't mean that if you are among robbers, you rob; if you are among evildoers, you do evil. But in the details of custom and practice, don't offend your neighbors by insisting that only your way is the right way. It is necessary to keep shalom even in someone else's bayit.□

STUDY QUESTIONS

1 Does *mishnah Pesachim* simply teach us, "When in Rome, do as the Romans do"? Are there limits on how far one can go in accommodating local custom? What are those limits?

2 Why did the dispersion of Jews throughout the Persian or Roman Empire effect the way Jews celebrated Passover and other festivals?

3 Does the *Mishnah* attempt to impose a single, uniform standard of ritual conformity upon all Jews everywhere? What provision do the rabbis make for differences of "custom"—as opposed to the binding standard of "law"?

4 What would the result be if Jews in each U.S. community celebrated Passover in a completely different way from Jews in other communities throughout the world? After several generations of this kind of diversity what would Passover be like? Would it be possible, under those conditions, for a Jew in Boston to celebrate Passover with a Jew in Paris, London, or Tel Aviv?

5 Why are the rabbis of the *Mishnah* so eager to avoid "conflict," even though they clearly prefer the "strictest rule"? Is there a contradiction here, or are the rabbis simply choosing between two equally desirable alternatives?

FOR DISCUSSION

Today, many Jews hold diverse views about not only the right way to observe Passover, but also about the right way to observe the Sabbath, the dietary laws, the rules of conversion, and many other issues. In fact, many communities advertise these differences by calling themselves "Orthodox," "Conservative," or "Reform," or in some cases, "Reconstructionist." We have come to accept (or at least to expect) such diversity, but how would the rabbis of the *Mishnah* have reacted to this subdivision of Judaism? Would they have been in favor of such differences, or would they have been opposed?

Having pondered that question—and assuming for the moment the role of a first or second century rabbi—how would you have prevented these differences from becoming institutionalized (or would you have)?

KETUBOTH 13 כתבות

MISHNAH 10 There are three countries as concerns marriage: Judea, Galilee, and beyond Jordan. A man may not move his wife—if she does not want to go—from one country to another. Within one country, he may move her from town to town, or city to city, but he may not move her from a city to a town, or a town to a city, if she does not want to move. He may take her from a bad dwelling to a good one, but not from a good dwelling to a bad one. Rabbi Simeon b. Gamaliel says: Not even from a bad dwelling to a good one if the move will do her harm.

THERE WAS NO EQUALITY of the sexes in ancient Israel. As in all societies until very recent times, the husband and father was the master of the household. However, that situation must have troubled the rabbis of the *Mishnah* because they kept adding more and more protections for the wife, each of which cut further into the absolute authority of the husband. While they continued to interpret Torah to give the husband first place in the family, they always added, "Yes, but. . . ."

Protection of the woman began even before a marriage took place. She could not be forced into marriage; she had to agree to the wedding. Then she had written protection in the marriage contract. If a woman was divorced, her husband had to return all the property she brought to the marriage (her dowry).

In their legal decisions in Roman times, the Jews divided the world into three parts: the two Jewish kingdoms of Judea and Galilee, and the Roman world. According to this *mishnah*, a wife could not be moved from one of these three areas to another without her permission. If the family was to be disrupted or upset, as a move from one country to another was bound to do, it could be done only by agreement between man and wife, said the rabbis.

Even more, they understood that a change in the quality of the place in which the family lived might be disruptive. People used to living in the country or in a small town might not be happy in the city, and vice versa. So any such move had to have the wife's agreement.

They went even further: The family that lived in a good house could not be moved to a less desirable house unless the wife agreed that it was necessary.

Rabbi Simeon wanted to go beyond even this. He said that a woman who was quite comfortable in a cottage might not want to move to a grander house — even though it might seem to be an upward move. Although Rabbi Simeon's decision was a minority judgment, it could be followed by a *dayan*, a judge, since all opinions in the *Mishnah* are valid.□

STUDY QUESTIONS

1 In what ways does *mishnah Ketuboth* reflect a concern for the wife's security and well-being? Do the rabbis place the wife's happiness *before* that of her husband?

2 Do the rabbis encourage the Jewish husband to think of himself as "lord and master" in his home? Did the Jewish wife retain any authority?

3 Why is it so important that a husband and wife agree on where they are to live? Can't they live in two different places at once?

And in the event that they do disagree, which one of them should decide whether they will move or not?

4 How would a present-day couple solve the problem of whether or not to move to another house or another city? Would they consider, first, whether the wife (or children) is going to be unhappy over the move, or are they likely only to consider whether the move will be advantagous to the husband's job or career?

If you were faced with this question, how would you resolve it? Which consideration (the wife's welfare vs. the husband's) would be most important for you?

5 How would a modern-day advocate of women's rights view the prescriptions of this *mishnah*?

6 In the Torah (*Genesis*, chapter 29) we read about Jacob's love for Rachel, and how willing he was to work seven years (and then seven years more after his uncle Laban cheated him) in order to earn the right to marry Rachel.

The Rabbis of *mishnah Ketuboth* never allude to this story, though it does, in fact, embody many of the same principles of conduct that this *mishnah* is concerned with teaching. The question is, which principles underlie both the *mishnah* and the Torah? Are all Jewish husbands expected to work seven (or even fourteen) years before they can marry their brides?

FOR DISCUSSION

Consider the following passage.

[KETUBOTH 8:] If a woman inherited goods before she was betrothed, the School of Shammai and the School of Hillel agree that she may sell them. . . .

They inquired before Rabban Gamaliel, "Since [the betrothed husband] gets possession of the woman, does he not get possession of her goods also?" He answered: "We are at a loss [to find a reason for giving him a right] over her new [possessions], and would you even burden us with the old also!"

Obviously, Rabban Gamaliel doesn't think a man is entitled to simply expropriate his wife's personal property—a very unusual judgment for its time! More importantly, this *mishnah* makes the point that a wife brings certain rights with her into marriage and never gives them up.

Now, what bearing does this discussion have on the later question of moving from one town to another?

EDUYOTH 1

MISHNAH 1   Shammai says: From this date; Hillel says: From that date. And the Sages say: It is not according to the opinion of either....

MISHNAH 2   (Shammai says) one kab of meal.... And Hillel says: Two kabs.... And the Sages say: It is a kab and a half....

MISHNAH 3   (Shammai says) one hin of drawn water.... Hillel says: nine kabs of water.... And the Sages say: It is not according to the opinion of either....

MISHNAH 4   Why do we record the opinions of Shammai and Hillel when these do not prevail? To teach the generations to come after that none should persist in his opinion, for lo, "the fathers of the world" (the writers of the Talmud) did not persist in their opinion.

EDUYOTH 1:1 TEACHES ONE of the most important lessons of the Jewish tradition. It says, in effect: The Torah was given by God and is thus perfect. And the Sages remind us that while it came from God, "the Torah was not given to angels." It was given to man—who is not perfect. Thus, no Jew can say with absolute certainty that this is what the Torah means. Perhaps another person's interpretation comes closer to the truth.

So the *mishnah* teaches us to be constantly aware that we may be mistaken, that the opinion of another may be valid.

Using the example of two of the greatest scholars of tradition, the *mishnah* shows that even they differed sharply on points of religious law, on interpreting the Torah. So what's the point of giving their opinions when these opinions have been reversed by the highest court? To teach us that hardest of lessons: I may be wrong.

This doesn't mean that all opinions are equally true. Nor does it mean that no matter how strongly you believe in your position, you should be ready to give it up. If you have seen suffering, you cannot accept another's opinion that there is no suffering. If you have seen injustice, you cannot accept the opinion that there is no suffering. The truths of your own eyes and your own heart are truths. However, in interpreting those truths, you are subject to error. Having seen the suffering and injustice, you are sure that they exist. But you cannot be as sure about why there is suffering, about who caused the injustice. These are interpretation.

Let your mind, your reason, be as open as your eyes, says this *mishnah.*□

STUDY QUESTIONS

1 In *mishnah Eduyoth*, Hillel and Shammai seem to disagree about everything. When two such learned and pious rabbis disagree so sharply upon so many questions of law, what does that tell us about the way in which the rabbis of the *Mishnah* arrived at their final judgments?

2 Does this *mishnah* really teach that all opinions are of equal value?

3 In a democratic society, debate has to remain open-ended, since no one person or party can be assumed to have all of the answers all of the time.

How does this principle of open-endedness apply to the *Mishnah*? Did the rabbis assume that they knew exactly how every generation, after their own, ought to follow the Torah?

4 What does it mean to "persist in one's opinion"? Shouldn't we insist on having our views heard — especially if we think we're right? What kind of "persistence" do you think the rabbis had in mind?

5 *Mishnah Eduyoth* provides only one means for later generations to overturn (or reverse) the opinions and rulings of the rabbis: that is, for a larger and a "wiser" rabbinic court to gather and reexamine both minority and majority views recorded in this (or any other) tractate of the *Mishnah*. After a careful deliberation, that larger and wiser court could, theoretically, change some or all of the *Mishnah's* legal judgments.

By insisting on this very deliberate and elaborate procedure, what were the rabbis trying to do? Were they simply trying to protect "tradition" by making it very hard to change any particular law, or were they actually encouraging later generations to review all of their inherited traditions systematically and periodically?

How do you interpret the intent behind this procedure?

6 How far can we go in reinterpreting or extending the laws of the Torah or the legal rulings of the *Mishnah*? Are we free, for example, to set aside any Biblical law that seems to us to be irrelevant or unacceptable to modern society? Are we free to add new laws where none exist in either the Torah or the *Mishnah*?

7 In the absence of a Sanhedrin or a *Bet Din* whose legal rulings would be regarded as binding by all Jews, where can Jews in the modern world turn for the kind of legal and ethical guidance that the rabbis of the *Mishnah* offered their generation?

FOR DISCUSSION

Let us assume that you and your classmates are all either followers of Hillel or followers of Shammai, and that you have been asked to reach a decision on a question of considerable importance to your community (e.g., whether or not to administer capital punishment, or run a turnpike through a residential neighborhood, or allow a job-producing industry which will pollute the air.)

Remembering the differences between the School of Hillel (which tended to be more liberal) and the School of Shammai (which tended to be stricter or more conservative in its judgments), try to conduct your debate in the manner of the Mishnaic Rabbis, and consider the following questions of procedure:

1. Will one side or the other be allowed to prevail, or will the opinions of both be noted (though not necessarily weighted equally)?

2. Will an impartial judge be asked to decide which side is "right" (i.e. which side has presented the most compelling arguments)?

3. Will the "losing" side be permitted to "persist" in its own opinion, or will it be obliged to accept the moral authority of the majority view—and act accordingly?

Printed in the USA
CPSIA information can be obtained
at www.ICGtesting.com
JSHW060048150824
68134JS00031B/2673